MW01232401

"*But I . . .*"
Said the Ego

A Guide to Strengthening Relationships
with Yourself and Others

ANDRÉ HILLS

authorHOUSE®

AuthorHouse™
1663 Liberty Drive
Bloomington, IN 47403
www.authorhouse.com
Phone: 1 (800) 839-8640

Published by AuthorHouse 07/10/2017

ISBN: 978-1-5246-9286-5 (sc)
ISBN: 978-1-5246-9285-8 (e)

Library of Congress Control Number: 2017908416

Print information available on the last page.

CONTENTS

CONTENTS

"BUT I..."

DEDICATION

I proudly stand on the shoulders of those that came before me and who gave me life: Mr. Charles D. Hills (my grandfather), Mrs. Naomi D. Hills (my grandmother) and Mrs. Juanita D. Hills Jenkins (my mother). I am truly blessed to have had the opportunity to experience such beautiful people whose lives shaped and created my own. Words could never express how much I value, owe and appreciate these individuals. I'm also dedicating this book to someone that came after me, my younger brother, Mr. James W. Jenkins, Jr. I love and appreciate him with my whole heart. Who he's become is the perfect balance between all that is and all that was.

My Mother's Rock

My grandfather, Charles D. Hills was my mother's rock and I chose these words because all I knew as a kid was that he never finished school and he couldn't read or write, but his baby girl (my mother) never wanted for anything. And if she did, he would be the first one there. I am eternally grateful that I got to experience such a man who would have such an enormous influence in my life. Up until the last day in his physical body, it was just he and I.

I remember it as if it was yesterday. I was in the eighth grade and it was the last day of school. In those days, we were required to bring a self-addressed envelope to school so our last report card of the year could be mailed home. "André," he said as I was walking out of the door to leave for school (when Charles Hills called your name, that meant "come to where I am"). When I walked into his bedroom, he was lying in the bed and he asked, "Do you have your envelope?" I replied, "Yes sir! I'll see you later!" As I headed toward the front door, I heard my name again and I ran back to the bedroom, this time a bit more rushed (my ride to school was waiting outside). He asked once again "Do you have your envelope?" I confirmed a second time, this time adding, "I gotta go, my ride is waiting!" He again said "OK." This happened one more time before I could get actually get out of the house.

We were all excited that day because we'd all be going to high school the following year. When I arrived back home, I walked in and called his name - "Granddaddy!" No response. I called out again and began walking through the house, going from room to room, looking for him... My grandfather had recently remodeled the house and although it wasn't a mansion, it was large enough to take an eighth grader several minutes to wander through. When I finally found him, my heart sank – he was lying on the floor in the guest room. The moment I saw him, I stopped and called his name again: "Granddaddy!" It was almost as if I was on autopilot; if you've ever experienced something similar, you understand how emotions and rational thought aren't always aligned. I thought to myself, "the doorbell is pretty loud, maybe if I go out and ring the doorbell, he'll wake up," so I did just that. After ringing it several times, I went to check to see if he was awake. He wasn't. I was in tears before I could make it back to the front door. I went outside on the porch, saw our neighbor and said "I think something is wrong with my granddaddy." From my appearance, she could tell something was very wrong and without saying a word, walked toward our house and went in. I couldn't move.

When I was growing up, the neighborhood was a tight-knit family – everyone knew everyone and everyone looked out for each other. When my neighbor came out of our house, she walked directly across the street to another neighbor's home and together, they walked back into my grandfather's house. I still couldn't move... When they both emerged, their nods provided the dreadful, heart wrenching affirmation that the worst had happened. The man who had been there for me every day of my life was no longer present in "this reality." From my 15-year old perspective, he died from a broken heart.

My Grandfather's Heart

My Mother – She was my grandfather's heart and my everything!

And not just *my* everything, but she was my older and younger brother's everything too.

It was November 16, 1998 in Statesboro, Georgia and my brothers and I were asleep. Suddenly, I was awoken by something… it felt as if I was hit by a truck. I couldn't figure out what it was and after a few minutes, the pain was gone. The strange thing was, it felt like a part of me had left with it. At 13 years old, I didn't know that was happening, but I knew something wasn't right. Instead of getting up, I laid there, staring at the ceiling and wondering. Time passed – first minutes, then hours – and I continued laying there, with the covers up to my neck, staring at the ceiling. I finally sat up and my stepfather happened to walk in the room. He asked, "what are you doing awake?" and I said "I know." He said "You know *what*?" and I repeated: "I know." My stepfather walked to my older brother's bed and woke him up. Understandably, he was startled and confused. The silently deafening, tense moments that followed were broken only by my stepfather's next words: "Your mother was in a car accident and she didn't make it." Shock set in – my brother and I both *heard* the devastating news, but it simply didn't make sense.

Several hours later, my grandmother and grandfather arrived at our house. Collectively, we decided it was best if we wait to break the news to my younger brother. But when we did, it hit him hard - our mother; our *everything* was gone.

A few weeks prior to her passing, she discovered that my stepfather had been having an affair. As distraught as she was and as easy as it could have been to remain in the situation, she instead sought a job opportunity in Savannah, our hometown. If successful, the position would serve as the foundation for she and my brothers and I to start anew. The following day, she called from Savannah and said, "I got the job and I'm coming back to get you guys." It was on her return trip that the terrible accident occurred.

After the news sunk in, my stepdad asked my brothers and I to sit down for a talk around the kitchen table. He asked "What are you guys going to do?" Note that he didn't say "we," he said "you guys". I spoke up first: "I am out of here!" "What do you mean?" he asked. I repeated my statement. At 13 years old, I realized two things: that the loss of our mother would change my life forever and that my brothers and I would possibly be separated.

My older brother decided to go live with our biological father, while my younger brother – who was too young to make a decision on his own – remained in the care of our stepfather, which was *his* biological father.

My mother was my everything, both during her life on earth and now as the angel that watches over me – over us. This book is dedicated to my mother – my grandfathers everything. Our everything.

It's in My Blood

One day, I was having a conversation with my coach and mentor, Mr. Herman Johnson, when he asked "What was the one event that had the most impact on your life?" I quickly asked, "Can it be more than one?" To which he replied, "Sure, but which ONE was most impactful?" I told him that I couldn't answer the question during that conversation - it was truly something I needed to put some more thought into.

I've often considered my mother's death to be the most impactful event in my life, but when I started digging deeper and giving it more consideration, another one came to mind.

By the time I was 17, I had saved up enough money to purchase my first car. It was a 1977 Oldsmobile Cutlass, black with red interior. One of the first things I promised myself I would do once I got my car was see my little brother in Statesboro, where he remained with my stepfather following my mother's accident.

I have to admit, I was a little nervous because of the distance. Savannah is only about an hour from Statesboro, but that was a big deal for a 17 year old. Still, I had to see my brother and I wasn't about to let a little nervousness get in the way. What I saw when I arrived is forever etched in my mind and would change me forever. My brother appeared as if no one was caring for him – his toes were coming out of the ends of his shoes and he badly needed a haircut. I used my excitement to mask the hurt I felt – he needed to see strength, not pain. We spent the day together and I hated to leave, but I had to return to Savannah. Overwhelmed with the sight of my brother in that condition, thoughts of my mother flooded into my brain. I cried the entire way home; my emotions pouring out of me uncontrollably all at once.

I remember telling myself over and over again, "THIS WILL NEVER HAPPEN AGAIN!" My brother deserved more and I was going to make sure that he was provided for. I used that experience to drive myself and focus on how I could create a life with him and for him. And wouldn't you know it, before long, my little brother and I were living together and supporting each other, right there in Savannah. I was happy and so was he!

At the time, I was working at a local toy store in the mall called K-B Toys to provide for my brother and I. I was a dedicated employee with a desire to succeed for my family. Eventually, I became the first person in the store's history to be promoted to an assistant manager prior to graduating high school. When I reflect on that time in my life, I'm reminded of how challenging it was. During and following high school, there were many 40-plus hour weeks. The balance of work and high school (and college soon thereafter) weighed heavily on me. Yet every time self-pity or sorrow crept in, I reminded myself of those words: "THIS WILL NEVER HAPPEN AGAIN!" As long as I had energy in my body, my brother would never want for anything.

When I turned 19, I was offered the position of Store Manager in Union City, just outside of Atlanta. I was excited at the opportunity, but before saying anything to my brother, I went to visit the store and the area to make sure it was a good fit for us (it was!). It ended up being a major next step in our lives – I signed a lease before leaving town and when I returned to Savannah, I told my brother about it, "I'm moving to Atlanta, do you want to stay here or would you like to come with me?" He said "I'm going with you!" and we moved the following week.

Our apartment was in College Park, Georgia and I vividly remember our first Christmas I had just turned 20 and a few weeks prior, my brother mentioned that he wanted a CD player for Christmas. All I could say was "OK" – believe it or not, I had no idea what CD player was, but I didn't my research and on Christmas night, I woke him up to open his presents (I couldn't wait!). The smile on his face upon seeing those gifts meant the world to me and I paused to take that moment in before heading to my room. When I got into my own bed, I began crying – not tears of sadness, mind you – I was so happy to see *his* happiness and the emotions of joy and relief overwhelmed me. With my head buried in my pillow and tears rolling down my cheeks, I said to myself, "It's in my blood." From my perspective as a 19-year old, I had seen my grandfather live and die for my mother. I had seen my mother live and die for her three children. And it was then that I realized that I was living – and would die – for my brother. I was committed to never stop giving him all I had to give.

Although my journey as a life coach has been fulfilling, it was quite challenging early on. I gave up everything – my home, cars, and an amazing job in the retail industry – to follow my dream as a life coach. It was an all or nothing decision and I had to be committed in order for it to be successful. One day, I received a call from my little brother, who said, "Hey, I know things are a little tough for you right now. Why don't you put your things in storage and come live with me." He had recently purchased his first home and because things were truly challenging, I swallowed my pride and accepted his generous offer.

Talk about a shift! My brother was now stepping up and providing me with the time and space to breathe for the first time in my entire life. In this time, I focused on developing and establishing my brand. I first began taking my life coaching business to multiple cities across the country and then expanded internationally. That progression of events serves as the building blocks for this very book. There have been so many ups and downs, all of which have strengthened my love and appreciation for my little brother and I also dedicate this book to him. I think it's safe to say that it's in his blood too.

A Grandmother's Love

They say there's nothing like a mother's love - and I agree. I can honestly say that I'm still relying on the unconditional love my brothers and I received from my mom. Next to a mother's love however, there's a grandmother's love. After my grandfather passed, my grandmother did not miss a beat; she left her home to come stay with me (in my grandfather's home). She was there for me in every way and I will always love and appreciate her for that. I would sit in the kitchen with her, as I did with my mother, just to keep her company, while she prepared breakfast and dinner. That's one thing that everyone knew - my grandmother *loved* cooking for us. Even on the weekends, she would wake everyone up to eat when breakfast was ready. She didn't care what we did after we ate (including going back to sleep), she just wanted to make sure we were never hungry.

In addition to keeping her company, sitting in the kitchen while my grandmother prepared meals was also a time for me to pay close attention to what she what she was doing - that's how I learned to cook. If you're from the South, you'll probably agree that our cuisine is an art form that requires a certain level of skill and years of practice to perfect – and believe me, my grandmother was a master of her craft. I still remember the little things, like when she would say "watch me - you have to measure the water with your finger...."

I can't mention by grandmother's cooking and not mention her famous "Jelly Layer Cake." It was the cake that she would literally take orders for and the one that everyone had to have during holidays and special occasions. It was her secret recipe: six thin layers of cake with apple jelly between each one. One day she shared her recipe with me and taught me how to make it. I felt both grateful and privileged because that meant I was the only one other than her that knew her secret. Then it happened - the orders would come in and she wouldn't have time to make all of them, so she would say, "I have to make a jelly layer for this person, this person, and this person - could you please make them for me?" I didn't mind at all - It was an honor and it was the least I could do after all she had done for me, my brothers and my cousins.

To write about all that my grandmother has done for me would be its own book. That's why I decided to write about the one thing that only she and I shared. She was truly the best grandmother anyone could ask for and for that reason, I dedicate this book to her. In my eyes, she embodied perfection in every way.

FOREWORD

by Mark (Maear) Arhin

Society has reached a place where the notion of individual, personal development has become increasingly prevalent. Combine this notion with the accessibility to information and exposure to knowledge and philosophies (of which there are more than ever) and it's easy to adopt an optimistic outlook when thinking of the direction that we're headed – both as individuals and as a society. I often see this in posts made by my friends and followers on social media, many of whom are sharing moments of enlightenment and motivation throughout their everyday lives. It almost feels like we have created a sort of Utopia.

Then I notice something else: the moment a so-called undesirable event occurs. Regardless of what you label it as, a moment of ignorance, arrogance or negativity – these things seem to occasionally creep into the lives of those very same enlightened people.

This is our current cycle of life and this is where André Hills represents himself as a true 21st-century thought leader. It's not every day such a unique and highly disciplined person enters your life or crosses your path and over the last year, I've had the pleasure of calling him both my friend and life coach.

When most of us find ourselves worrying about future events or enduring the seemingly endless doldrums of day-to-day life, André is living in a state of joyful bliss. But how?...Quite simply: he won't have it any other way. Never have I seen a man be so disciplined in exercising an ongoing commitment to identifying and overcoming negativity. André specializes in the practice of embodying positivity, which is why abundance, happiness and mental, spiritual and emotional well-being orbit him, as if the reality he has created for himself has its own gravitational pull.

When André said he was writing a book, I knew it would be great. Within these pages, you'll find that missing link to your happiness and the primary source to society's current disconnect. For example: why do we find ourselves in a constant state of emotional flux? On Sunday, we're on top of the world and can't be stopped and then on Tuesday, we're fighting an uphill battle of negative thoughts. These two mindsets – the peaceful and the embattled – are within all of us and it's the reason society finds itself in a constant, polarizing state of "me vs. you." Our egos are the source from which our reactions to positive and negative events come. Our egos drive our needs: to be right, to be acknowledged, to be accepted, to be heard, to prove others wrong. In the face of reality, our egos have become adept at distracting us with the perceived, limiting our potential to make the most of our current situation and hindering personal and interpersonal growth.

This book is the product of decades of personal life experiences and its purpose is to uncover the truth about the internal and external conflicts created by our egos. You'll be exposed to simple, methodical approaches to understanding how to grow as a person, how to establish better relationships and how to maintain a balanced mental, spiritual and emotional outlook. You'll learn to identify with your loving nature, which will lead you to the true meaning in your life. This book will be your doorway to true happiness and coexistence, while introducing you to a healthy mindset that will launch positive discussions and create flourishing relationships. This will be one of the most revolutionary and empowering pieces of literature that you will ever read.

Special Thanks

My Clients

I would like to thank all of my past, present and future clients. Being a life coach is my life's calling and I'm fortunate to have had the opportunity to make a difference in the lives so many individuals around the globe – for that, I am incredibly thankful. In my efforts to help others, I have learned that the most rewarding aspect of my job comes in the form of what my clients provide me, and that is to expose me to new situations and mindsets, all of which have indirectly contributed to making me a better life coach and person. So to everyone that I have had the opportunity to coach – whether it was a one-on-one session or at workshop – I say thank *you* from the bottom of my heart.

My Mentor

I would like to give a special thanks to my coach, mentor and friend: Mr. Herman Johnson. I first met Herman in 2000 in Atlanta, where I managed a store at Cumberland

Mall (American Eagle Outfitters, which if you've been to a mall within the past 20 years, you've probably seen one). At the time, Herman was a district manager for the company and he happened to be at my store for a visual workshop that was attended by a host of other store managers. We had a brief interaction and I'll never forget his words: "be careful, you never know who will be your boss," and although I understood the statement on face value, I didn't think anything of it. And because I didn't know him, I never thought that comment would have had anything to do with me.

Shortly after - Herman transferred to the Atlanta area and his office just so happened to be in the store that I was managing. For 10 years, Herman was my supervisor, but his role in my life was infinitely greater. His influence helped mold me into the person I am today.

At *exactly* the 10-year mark, Herman came to the store I was managing (now in Chattanooga, Tennessee). Shortly after arriving at the store, he came to me and said, "let's take a walk." We conversed, made idle chit-chat and then he dropped this on me: "I'm going to ask you a question: do you know why you're here?"

Herman has a way with words and I knew the question was deeper than it sounded. I replied "yes," and the next statement he made was one that shifted things for me forever. He said, "When are you going to stop using your job to do what you know you're supposed to be doing?" That was the end of the conversation. My professional success in retail was a direct result of my ability to focus on the individuals and teams in the nine different stores that I worked closely with for a decade. And as someone who understands and appreciates the correlation between effective leadership and success, Herman was indirectly challenging me to do what I was born to do.

Within a year after he asked that question and made that powerful statement, I started my own private practice as a life coach. I was no longer using my job as a channel for my true calling. I began *living* it. And I have a tremendous amount of gratitude and appreciation for Herman Johnson for inspiring me to be the best that I could be. Even today, Herman is still in my life as *my* coach, mentor and friend.

My Mentee

I never would have predicted that my mentee – Michael Touchton – would still be in my life contributing all that he is. Interestingly, I also met Michael at American Eagle Outfitters in 2004, when I was managing the Towne Center location in Kennesaw, Georgia. I hired Michael when he was 18 years old. He always seemed to have something going on in his personal life that affected his performance at work. One could refer to him as my "problem child" - but I saw something in him. After some time, Michael became my stockroom supervisor, but even then, there were plenty of times where I was picking up his slack and protecting him from my boss (and my bosses' boss). But that "something"

I saw in him was always there and I made a conscious decision to invest in him. Whenever I really needed him, he was there; I remember many times we would have a corporate visit, which required longer-than-normal shifts (often overnights or early mornings), and Michael would always stay until the work was done. A far cry from being my "problem child" today, Michael now works for a major financial PR firm and has used his skills to help me take my company to another level. Not only was he responsible for getting my first article published with *Moneyinc.com* - he's actually the editor of this book.

Investing in another person is an amazing experience and it always has a way of coming full circle. Herman invested in me, I invested in Michael and it all started at American Eagle Outfitters. I couldn't have a special thanks section in this book and not include this guy. After all these years, I'm so very grateful that he is in my life investing in me as I did him. Many thanks!

The Inspiration

It's January 2017 and like clockwork, my phone rang at 6:30 a.m. on a Monday. On the other end of the line is my mentee, business partner and friend, Mark Arhin; he's calling from London. A client of mine was friends with Mark and it was through this connection that we met. Each Monday, he and I connected to catch up and discuss the day-to-day occurrences of our respective businesses.

It was during one of these Monday conversations with Mark that I noticed I was feeling a little "off." This self-awareness of feelings – which is something I have long emphasized with my clients – was something I was now putting into practice. I said to Mark, "it seems like the majority of our conversations have been about how my company and can benefit yours, instead of how our companies can be mutually beneficial and in this moment, and I'm not feeling good about that."

The strongest friendships are based on honesty and Mark and I have an agreement that we will be up front with one another, regardless of the situation. After my comment, Mark acknowledged how I was feeling and went on to assure me that my company was indeed at the forefront of this thoughts and ideas. We ended the call, but I was still not feeling great about the conversation. This was the very first conversation between Mark and I that ended on somewhat of a disconnected note.

After the conversation with Mark, I decided to do something to distract myself from my feelings, so I decided to shave and cut my hair. Despite my attempt to distract myself, I still felt off. I found myself thinking "this relationship means too much to me for me to be feeling this way, so I'm just going to stop focusing my thoughts on this." Because as someone who always practices being present and in-the-moment, it's important that I constantly guard my thoughts.

I learned this practice from "The Power of Now" by Eckhart Tolle (if you haven't read it, I suggest you do so – right after you finish this one). It's a small, simple phrase, but it seemed to be doing most of the work. That's when I had an epiphany! I looked at my reflection in a mirror and said: "OH SHIT - IT'S MY EGO" – *that's* what's driving the "but I" mindset.

It was in that very moment that I knew that this experience – which is so relatable and universal – should be shared with others: "But I, said the Ego."

In teaching the law of attraction, one of the most common conversations that I have with clients is about the gap between when you make things happen and when you wait for the inspiration to act. I made a note of this gap and you'll find more details about it in the Intro, but that message is woven throughout this book and is one I learned about this from the teaching of Abraham Hicks. It offered me another way to do what I love to do, which is help others become the best versions of themselves possible. This book will help you become more present in the now and enjoy the journey, all while building better relationships. I hope you enjoy!

INTRODUCTION

Years ago, a very close friend and I were talking and it was in that conversation that I was introduced to the concept of "the Ego." In that discussion, my friend suggested that I was speaking through my Ego and although I didn't agree with it at the time, I now understand what he was saying. I disagreed because I lacked the clear understanding of what the Ego – my Ego – was.

Since then, I have spent a great deal of my career analyzing and evaluating the Ego. Equipped with the essential understanding of what it is and the influence it has on my everyday life, I now look back and recognize many things I would have done differently in past relationships. Does that mean I have regrets? Not at all. It simply means that I appreciate the clarity that these experiences have offered me.

My job as a life coach is not to necessarily teach my clients anything; it's to provide a frame of reference so that when anything happens – from the trivial to the profound (and everything in between) – they can say "Ohhh, *that's* what he meant! Now I get it!" And believe me, this happens all the time. Needless to say, my realization of my own Ego's voice was *my* time to say "Ohhh, *that's* what he meant! I get it now!"

When you finally recognize and separate yourself from your Ego, you start reacting and making decisions from a different place - from your heart and not my head. And once you become more aware of your Ego and how it operates, I guarantee that it will create more positive life experiences on many levels. You see, your Ego tries its best to protect the false-made self, which is who you *think* are you versus who you *really* are.

Some powerful questions to ask yourself are: Who am I? What are my true intentions? To love, to be kind, to support and understand? As you continue to read this book, it's important for you to understand that is was not written to give you specific advice, but to offer you a different perspective; one that will lead to a better relationship with yourself and with others.

In one way or another, every chapter is an extension of my own personal experiences, because it is through those experiences that I learned to become aware. And in sharing those with you, I hope it will do the same. In other words, this book is more about awareness than anything else. Adopt this mindset and watch it transform your relationships. You will begin appreciating others for being exactly who they are, exactly *where* they are, and you'll develop a newfound sense of personal stability.

The Ego is only an illusion, but a very influential one. Letting the Ego-illusion become your identity can prevent you from knowing your true self. Ego, the false idea of believing that you are what you have or what you do, is a backwards way of assessing and living life.

-*Wayne Dyer*

Chapter 1

"But I..."

"...am always the one," said the Ego

"It's me - it's always me. It's always been me!"

"If it weren't for me, nothing would ever happen."

"And even when you do try, something *always* seems to go wrong..."

Wow - OK, hold up - wait!

These are a lot of thoughts to think all at once.

They're also a lot of words for someone to hear – all at once.

And to think, it all began with one thought - that whisper you heard saying ***but I***.

Sound familiar?

Have you heard that whisper?

I'm sure you have.

We all have.

So the question is this: are you really *feeling* this way or is your Ego that's feeling this way and trying to pull you in?

The better question: is "what you're hearing" even true?

Probably not.

Think about it. "If it weren't for me, **nothing would ever happen**."

Seriously?

That could not be further from the truth – In fact, that couldn't possibly be true.

Yet it's something that you're lead to believe.

First there's the whisper, then the feeling(s), then the *false* truth.

And the false truth is connected to your false self.

Otherwise known as: your Ego.

The reality is, if there's no one literally making you do something.

You are doing all that you do because you *want* to do it.

This may be a little hard to hear and accept, but it's the truth.

Interestingly enough, that voice inside your head - your Ego…

It's usually silent during the doing.

In other words, your Ego doesn't start to speak until things turn out differently than you would have hope for or believed.

And when this happens, it needs someone to blame - as if you didn't have a choice.

Crazy right?

Simply put, if you're feeling like you're "always the one," then you're *choosing* to be the one.

If you want a different result, it's time to do something different.

Moving forward, I strongly encourage you to do what you do simply because you *want* to do it.

Remember: you always have a choice.

You can choose to let go of the expectation as it relates to **how you think others should respond** to your doing…

Or you can choose to allow your Ego –to convince you that you're "always the one."

Here's the problem with always thinking you're the one:

- It leaves you feeling like others are not doing anything.

- It leaves you feeling like others don't care.

- It leaves you feeling like you should stop doing all that you do, which could actually be the complete opposite of what you really want (or even what's best for you).

- It leads you to compare what you do to what others are doing (or not doing).

So what are some solutions?

- Be aware - listen **for** the voice, not **to** the voice.

- Accept that people are different and may act and respond differently than you.

- When in doubt, ask questions - it's the only way you would really know.

- Don't assume - express yourself more freely and with respect.

Full disclosure: there will be times when you're "always the one."

However, it's critically important that you understand that you're doing things because you *want* to. Your Ego will do its best to convince you that it's unfair and that you have no choice; this is what it does to protect itself (and we'll discuss this later).

But believe me: you *always* have a choice.

"The greatest conflicts are not between two people but between one person and himself."

- Garth Brooks

Chapter 2

"But I..."

"...don't care," said the Ego

You don't? Oh ok...

So the moments you found yourself saying this out loud, when no one was around - who were you talking to? And if there were other negative emotions involved, I'm sure it may have sounded a little different...

Maybe something like "I don't give a fuck!" Right?
Same thing - and yet the question remains - who were you talking to?
I'll tell you: it was a conversation between you and your Ego. Think about, there was no one else around. Your Ego was doing what Egos do. In this case, it was trying to convince

you that you don't care about something or someone, when you really do.

"I care about what others think" our words usually go unspoken unless a person is directly asked. What do I mean?

People usually find it challenging to admit that they care as much as they actually do - not only *about* others, but what others *think*.

This is something I experience often as a life coach. I have had many coaching sessions where I could feel that caring too much about what others think was at the root of what the client was feeling.

But they never admit that own their own.

For instance, after a client finishes expressing to me what they are currently experiencing or "going through," I might say something like "I'm hearing you say that you really care about what others think and that's what's holding you back - would that be an accurate statement?"

Then the client hesitates before reluctantly affirming.

"Yes."

Now, it's after the "yes" that I allow them space to process hearing themselves say that – for some, it's the first time they've ever admitted it. Then I might say "talk to me about how you're feeling right now."
99% of the time, they feel emotional.

So do you really care what others think or does your Ego?

Without a doubt, your Ego wants to be liked. It wants to fit in and be accepted. Who you really are wouldn't get too caught up with what others think, because you know that when you follow your instincts - your heart - there will be people who don't like it. That's normal. That's healthy.

More importantly, you know that there will always be people who don't understand. That's also normal. That's also healthy. After all, not everyone knows your heart, instinct or even your dream.

In the last chapter, I mentioned awareness. In addition to that, I highly encourage you not to **hold others accountable** for something they **could not fully understand**. It doesn't matter how many words you use to try to make them understand – sometimes they just won't.

Here are the problems with caring too much:

- It will slow down your own momentum.

- It will lead you in a direction for which you have no desire.

- It will confuse you.

- It will dictate your decisions and choices.

- It will leave you feeling unfulfilled and resentful.

So what are some solutions?

- Get clear about what you really want and go after it, regardless of what other maybe thinking or saying.

- Develop the ability to hear what others have to say and decide if and how you may be able to benefit.

- Trust your instincts.

- Become comfortable with making decisions and choices that are best for **you**.

- Care about yourself as much (or more) as you care about what others think.

What I'm not saying: that you should not consider what others have to say - especially those that love you.

What I am saying: that no one could possibly know how you're truly feeling but you.

The ultimate aim of the Ego is not to see something, but to be something.

- Muhammad Iqbal

Chapter 3

"But I..."

"...remember," said the Ego.

"But I remember what happened the last time," said the Ego.

I'm sure you do - and the message here is not to encourage you to forget that. However, it is more productive to focus on what's happening *now* than to continue focusing on what has already happened.

Think about it. If that thought – "But I remember what happened the last time" – becomes actual words you exchange with someone, it becomes as much about you as it is them. And your Ego wouldn't have it any other way.

What it says about you is you're stuck in the past. What it simply says about them is that they did something that didn't please you in the past.

So when the Ego says "I remember," it's usually connected to not wanting to feel disappointed or let down again. It's trying to protect itself from the hurt or pain that could be associated with another's behavior. If you're present in the moment enough to hear the Ego say "I remember" - this could mean that you may have trust issues that may or may not have anything to do with the other person.

This may be an opportunity for you to have a different type of conversation that could lead to you to making choices that you feel are best, without being stuck in the past.

Consider this - do you think the Ego would ever say, "But I remember when you did that thing that made me very happy"? No, because it has no reason to protect itself from an occurrence from which there was a positive outcome. As mentioned earlier, when the Ego says "I remember," it's usually connected to trying to protect its identity, while waiting patiently for the moment it can point the finger or place the blame on someone else; All the while preventing you from looking at yourself. You see, to the Ego, it could never be *you* - it would have to be *them*.

Here are the problems with being stuck in the past:

- It can cause you to be unfair to others by not giving them the opportunity to act differently, but more importantly, be different – the person they are now, not was.

- You will be subconsciously attracting more of the same behavior from others and then blame them for that behavior instead of understanding that it's really you.

- It will give others the perception that you want them to be different from who they really are, creating or amplifying insecurities for them.

- You'll hold grudges without even realizing it, because you are basing your current actions on their past actions.

So what are some solutions?

- Have honest conversations about the way you're feeling.

- Be fair to others and give them a chance.

- Be fair to yourself.

- Understand that all that has happened is **done**. That means there's nothing anyone can do to change it.

- Forgive yourself and forgive others.

We must go beyond the constant clamor of

Ego, beyond the tools of logic and reason,

to the still, calm place within us: the realm of the soul.

- Deepak Chopra

Chapter 4

"But I..."

"...feel," said the Ego.

"But I feel like you should be doing something differently," said the Ego.

This is truly a very tricky one, but one that is equally important to understand.

Why?

Because usually when the Ego says this, what it really means is that you want others to do what *you* want them to do - or what *you* feel is best...

Hmmm...

You're probably thinking, "That's not me..."

"I don't care..."

"...they can do whatever they want to do."

Let me go on the record: on the surface, you may not be too far off base.

However, if you take a look at what's REALLY happening here...

Although it may seem as if it's you versus someone else and what they may or may not be doing, it's not – yet again, it's you versus you.

It's you versus your Ego –

(Note: below is me "talking" as if I was having a conversation with someone about this)

"Oh, I'm beginning to understand..."

If they were doing something different, you would feel better?

"OK, it's becoming clearer..."

If they were doing something different, it would make YOU happy?

"That's it!"
So what you're saying is that it's *their* job to ensure *you're* happy?
You see what's happening here, right?
All that is about the Ego - it is the Ego!

As I'm sure you know and have heard many times before, It's not up to anyone to make you happy - happiness is an inside job.

That being said, the question becomes:
Do you have the right to feel that someone else should be doing something differently?

Before you answer that...

Don't mistake it - On the surface, it may look as if doing what you feel they should be doing is the best thing – the only logical thing.

However, it's important to know that although someone's choices and decisions may speak to something different - the reality is that no one knows themselves like they do. No one can truly understand what they are going through like they can - no matter how many times it's explained.

So - are we really having a conversation about what someone is doing or not doing?

Or are we in fact having a conversation about communication and respect?

Because that's what it boils down to: communication and respect –

...Now, the Ego is not trying to hear that!

The Ego is all about "self" -

"Me – Me – Me – Me – Me..."

Now - take a couple of seconds to reflect on your past relationships.

And now think about your current ones.

You're beginning to understand and see things a little differently, right?

You may even thinking,
"Damn, I fucked that up!"
Well, it is what it is now…
…all you can do from this point is make a conscious decision to be more aware.

Of course, you can always go back and apologize, if you feel it's necessary. Because I can promise you that it wasn't all them, as your Ego lead you to believe.

What I'm encouraging you to do when you hear your Ego say this, is to look at it as an opportunity to truly connect with others - to be *that one* to ask how *they* are really feeling. Be *that one* that let others know that although you may not understand - even disagree, you're still for here for them. If they need to talk or someone to listen, you're here.

Believe me, that would mean the world to a person that's going through a difficult time.

Remember: No matter how close you are, you never know what someone is going through. The key is for you to make it more about them instead of allowing your Ego to make all about you. It's an opportunity to show love – to be love.

Here are the problems with thinking that others should be acting differently:

- It can cause you to push others away.

- It can cause you to focus less on being a better friend or partner.

- You may become less aware of and attentive to others' needs.

- It can cause you to miss out on being a part of some important moments and milestones with those you love and care about.

So, what are some solutions?

- Try to be as understanding as possible.

- Be patient and willing to hang in there...

- Be willing to really listen to the other person.

- Recognize the other person's needs and be supportive, without losing who you truly are.

"The Ego is the false self-born out

of fear and defensiveness."

– *John O'Donohue*

Chapter 5

"But I..."

"...already," said the Ego.

"But I already said that," said the Ego.

To put myself out there, this is something I hear my Ego say often.

To be entirely candid, I really don't enjoy repeating myself (and who does?).

I want to know that I'm being listened to and I want to know that what I have to say is valuable enough for you to pay attention.

Did you notice what just happened as I shared my truth? I was spouting:

"I... I... I..."

Does this resonate with you?

Make no mistake – I'm communicating my feelings appropriately, but even though these statements are true, no healthy and productive relationship is founded on either person feeling like it's all about themselves, intentional or unintentional – it **will** backfire at some point.

In the grand scheme of things, what does it matter if someone doesn't remember *exactly* what you said?
Sure, you may have to repeat yourself, but does that mean others are not listening? Absolutely not.
It may simply mean they have forgotten.

Or maybe they didn't want to hear what you had to say in the first place.
Maybe what you have to say isn't as important as you think – which may be hard to accept, since it always seems to be about you.

As mentioned in the previous chapters, this is more about you than it is about them. Remember, your Ego has to have someone to blame. Its job is to make a big deal out of something that's not a big deal at all. Instead of doing most of or all of the talking, try focusing on having a more balanced conversation - more balanced relationships; one that includes you asking more questions and really listening to what the other person has to say.

Question - When *you* didn't remember, did *they* make a big deal about it?

Probably not.

And even if what *you* had forgotten was important to them, did you want them to understand that you simply forgot?

Probably so.

Simply put, it's not all about you, even though your Ego will never stop trying to get you to believe that.

Here are the problems with making it all about you:

- You may believe others are not listening to you.

- You may believe that others don't "get it."

- You may feel like others don't care at all.

- You may become frustrated.

- You may become suspicious that others are trying to manipulate you.

So, what are some solutions?

- Understand that there is a chance that you weren't as clear as you thought.

- Understand that, while others may have heard what you said, they may need clarification on what you meant.

- Understand that others "get it" in their own time.

- Accept that everyone has the right to feel however they feel, even if you don't understand.

Letting go of your Ego opens the door to taking

a new and creative course of action.

– *Suzanne Mayo Frindt*

Chapter 6

"But "I..."
"...need," said the Ego

"But I need things to be different, "said the Ego.

Reread that sentence then take about a minute to think about it.

Have you ever thought that or even gone so far as say that to someone?

If you have, what are you really saying and how is your Ego connected to that "situation"?

What you're really saying is that your happiness is conditional. I learned this from the teaching of Abraham Hicks.

In order for you to be happy, you "need" the conditions to be a certain way. And I'm sure you know by now, the Ego is right there with you - or should I say, you are right there with it?

This doesn't mean you should not express yourself to those you are in a relationship with at any level, however, I am encouraging you to listen for this thought - this subtle whisper. If you find that this is something that you hear often, the question becomes: is it you or is it your Ego?

If this is something you hear often, this could only mean that you need it be another way – *your* way – more often. I definitely encourage you to give this one some thought. If you are a person that always wants it your way, I'm sure this will become a problem at some point, if it hasn't already. Maybe it's time to become more aware and be more willing to compromise two qualities that are extremely important in every relationship.

Believe me, your Ego is making it about the other person when in fact, it's more about you. Please understand that in spite of what you were conditioned to believe, happiness is a choice - one that you can choose regardless of what others are doing or saying. Take a minute to process what you've just read and then ask yourself: what do I really need?

If you need something to be different, then it's up to you make it different. Have you ever thought about why you haven't initiated the change to make things different? More often than not, the answer is "no" and that's likely because it's considered difficult or challenging - yet you want other people to do whatever they have to do in order for *you* to feel better. And you want them to do it as soon as possible.

Sound familiar? I'm sure it does. If it's you who needs things to be different or feel differently, it's up to *you* to make it happen – no one else. Don't allow your Ego to set unrealistic expectations for the people you love and care about. It will set you up for failure and disappointment every time.

Here are some problems with needing things to be different:

- It causes selfishness.

- It can cause you to be dismissive.

- It can cause you to become disconnected.

- It can lead you to believe that your needs don't matter to others.

- It can lead you to believe your happiness is connected to what others may be doing or saying.

- It can cause you to begin to care less about others in general.

So, what are some solutions?

- Be willing to compromise.

- Understand that, regardless of the relationship, it truly takes two.

- Focus more on understanding others.

- Despite what you think you need, understand that the approval of others is not one of them.

- Be open to hearing the ideas of others.

- Be open to try new things, even if it maybe outside your comfort zone.

- Make it about the person, not the thing.

- Make feeling good the priority.

When Ego is lost, limit is lost. You become infinite, kind, beautiful.

- *Yogi Bhajan*

Chapter 7

"But I..."

"....am different," said the Ego

Of course you are.

This is something you've known from a young age.

So what does it really mean when your Ego slips this one in?

If this is what your Ego is telling you or trying to get you to believe, it usually equates to you not feeling good enough. Besides, the Ego has to protect itself from the possible hurt and disappointment. And believe it or not - as you may be thinking this has everything to do with someone else, it doesn't. It's all you. It's about you accepting who you are and loving who you are!

To help put things in perspective, the Ego usually says this when you are interested in someone you feel may not be interested in you. And the interesting thing is, when you hear that voice say *"but I..."*, you instantly forget about how you met that person; how fun and unexpected it was; and how you were both eager and excited to exchange numbers and were looking forward to seeing each other again.

That excitement lasts until you open that door and invite the Ego in. And this happens the moment you start to think - or should I say **over**-think. This is why being aware of your thoughts and understanding that you always have a choice is important.

You can choose what you focus on and I encourage you to focus what feels best. Because if you choose to focus on what your Ego is telling you, it will lead to more and more thoughts that will drive your insecurities. "I wonder if he or she really likes me?"; "I haven't worked out in a while, so

I wonder what she or she will think of my body?"; and so on and so forth....

Abraham Hicks, author of "Ask and it is Given" says "...it only takes 17 seconds" for similar thoughts to be added." Think about it. Your Ego knows that it only has to get you started and you will do the rest, while distracting you from the realization that the only person that you need to feel good enough for is *you*.

Here are the problems with not feeling good enough:

- It can cause insecurity.

- It will lead to self-doubt.

- It can cause you to be non-responsive.

- It can cause you to focus on what's really not important, while missing what *is*.

So, what are some solutions?

- Stay present in the moment.

- Ignore the "what ifs".

- Be more intentional as it relates to what you focus on.

- Focus more on loving and accepting yourself.

Apologizing does not always mean that you're wrong and the other person is right. It just means that you value your relationship more than your Ego. - *Unknown*

Chapter 8

"But I..."

"...am right," said the Ego

"But I am right," said the Ego. This is a BIG one!

Once you become more aware of the Ego, you'll realize that the Ego **ALWAYS** feels the need to be right.

This is why it's extremely important for you to become more aware and separate yourself from your Ego.

Because if you don't, this very thing will keep you from building long-lasting, meaningful relationships.

So, really think about it for a second - do you really want to be right all of the time?

Or is it your Ego that wants to be right?

This is the final chapter, so by now I'm sure you know the answer.

The real questions become, now that you know what you know, does the answer resonate with you?

Do you have a better understanding of what the Ego is and how it operates?

Think about the times when you knew you were right about something. I mean right without a doubt, undeniably right. And as you continued having a conversation with the other person, who was trying to convince you otherwise, you realized you were actually wrong all along.

Do you remember feeling that tug - between voices?

One saying "oh shit, they're right!" - and the voice saying "they may be right, but you don't have to admit it - just don't say anything. After all you've said in efforts of making your case, you'll just look like a fool."

And there it is - your Ego is in now in protection mode - trying to protect your image again.

Here are some problems with needing to be right all the time:

- You can become defensive.

- You may devalue others' opinions.

- You may discredit or minimize others.

- You can become dismissive and push others away.

So, what are some solutions?

- Understand that every situation is not about being right or wrong.

- Recognize the value in what others say - and know that what they say is valuable to them.

- Give others the respect you want or require.

- Be more considerate to how others may feel.

- Listen. Listen. Listen.

Love doesn't break hearts egos do - *Unknown*

Now what?

THE EGO CHALLENGE

Note from the Author:

If I had to choose one word that would speak directly to purpose of this book, that word would be awareness. As you've probably gathered from all that you've read, once you become aware of your Ego, it would better the relationship you have with yourself – as well as others. Before now, you could have labeled the Ego as a bad thing. Now hopefully you can see no matter if it's referred to as good or bad, you know that being aware it can help you become a better person – be a better person.

While in the process of writing this book, I thought it would be a great idea to stay connected with the readers. Then I thought, in addition to staying connected to them, I'd also like to find out which chapter in this book resonated the most with them and why? In addition, now that they will be more aware, what else have they heard their Ego say? Which relationships specifically has improved? How has being aware improved those relationship? So that's when I came up with **The Ego Challenge.**

The Ego challenge is ultimately about the new found awareness and the shifts in your relationships because of it.

With that being said, I are excited to mention that there will be another book - **"But I" said the Ego (Volume II)** that will be crafted around the experiences of 8 individuals.... That's right!"

This is how it works.

1. **Submit an email** that includes your thoughts of this book. How has it helped you? What were your biggest takeaway(s)? Also include what you heard your Ego say since you've read the book and how has that helped you? What relationships have improved because of your new found awareness?

2. **INCLUDE THE DETAILS** – as mentioned earlier, the experiences that are chosen will be included in the next book!

3. **Speak directly with the Author!** Shortly after submitting your email, you will be asked to schedule a time to speak with me directly about your submission. This will allow you the space and time to go into more details and all

Submit your email to egochallenge@andrehills.com by September 1, 2017 to be considered for Volume II, which is planned to be released in spring 2018.

If you are reading this book after September 1, 2017, it's not too late! You can still be considered for other volumes. You will be able to find the details for the other volumes on my website in the future at www.andrehills.com - be sure to visit the website today and sign up for our newsletters so you'll be guaranteed not to miss it.

Thanks for reading!

Printed in the United States
By Bookmasters